101 Uses For A PUG

WILLOW CREEK PRESS®

Published by Willow Creek Press, Inc.
P.O. Box 147, Minocqua, Wisconsin 54548

Design: Donnie Rubo
Printed in China

Little known quirky Pug uses...

Nose warmer

Foot warmer

Palm reader

Washcloth

Someone who has your back...

...and makes sure your cappuccino isn't too hot.

Bedmate

Mattress

Couch potato

Dreamcatcher

Totem pole

Monument

Someone to laugh
at your jokes...

...and to comfort you.

Peeping Tom

Spy

Hugger   Kisser

Valentine

Security alarm

Backseat driver

Confidant

Drinking buddy

Someone who waits for you...

...and always looks up to you.

Protagonist

Antagonist

Benchwarmer

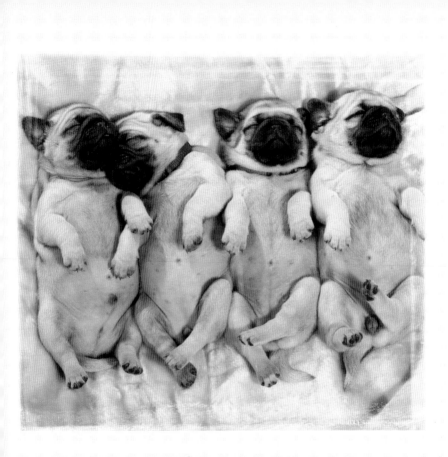

Bed warmer

Beach bum

Yard ornament

Pugs make great workers too.
They're whizzes at jobs like...

Entrepreneurs

 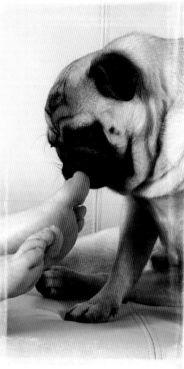

Manicurist   Pedicurist

Seamstress

Cobbler

Dancer

Model

Logger

Loan shark

Table busser

Dishwasher

Florist

Babysitter

Guard

Greeter

Optometrist

Proctologist

Therapist

Philosopher

Artist

Woodworker

Pack mule

Hiking guide

Pugs are great with household chores like...

Arborist

Gardener   Lawn mower

Pool boy

Towel boy

Interior decorator

Computer expert

Shovel

Snowplow

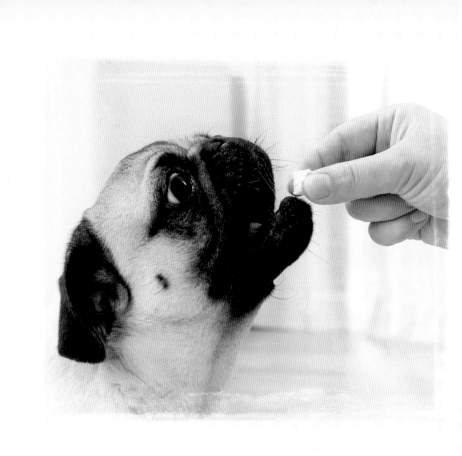

Taste tester

Food critic

The sophisticated Pug might be a ...

Zen master

Tour guide   Musician

Diva

Hipster

Fashionista

Fashion accessory

The athletic Pug might be a...

Life guard

Trailblazer

Athletic trainer

Horse
whisperer

Dog
trainer

Olympic gymnast

Sprinter   Swimmer

Wrestler

Sports fan

Cyclist

Deckhand

Teammate

Goalie

Bungee-jumper

Skateboarder

Not to be overlooked uses...

Party animal

Clown   Easter Bunny

Christmas gift

Santa Claus   Elf

89

Epicure

Shoeshiner

Crowd control

Attack dog

Cargo

Vice grips

Your best friend